THE
UNKNOWN CATHEDRAL

Lesser known aspects of
St Magnus Cathedral in Orkney

Edited by Steve Callaghan and Bryce Wilson

Orkney Heritage

Published by Orkney Islands Council
School Place, Kirkwall, Orkney.

First published in 2001
ISBN 0-9540320-0-4 (Hardback)
ISBN 0-9540320-1-2 (Softback)

Printed by The Orcadian Limited,
Hell's Half Acre, Hatston, Kirkwall, Orkney

The publishers wish to thank The Ness Robertson Trust,
The Society of the Friends of St Magnus Cathedral and The Robertson Trust
for financial support which made possible the production of this volume

CONTENTS

Earl Rognvald. Stanley Cursiter's design for Reynold Eunson's carving in the St Rognvald Chapel.

THE FOUNDER, ST ROGNVALD

Ron Ferguson

St Magnus is Orkney's patron saint, and most people in Orkney know quite a bit about him. We hear less about St Rognvald. I think that's a pity, because he is a very interesting character.

St Magnus is an awesome character: his gentleness and saintliness shine down through the ages. Rognvald is an earthier, more robust character: and while I can admire Magnus and his sacrifice, I personally find Rognvald to be a more congenial character.

Rognvald was a charismatic adventurer, a warrior, a romancer, a poet, a song writer, a musician, a man of action and bravery, a man of his word, a man of God, a pilgrim. Above all, he was the man who had the vision of founding this Cathedral in memory of his martyred uncle, Magnus. He not only dreamed about it, he made it happen. For this, he can be forgiven much.

He was born Kali Kolsson, and was brought up in Southern Norway. Here is what the *Orkneyinga Saga* says of Kali as a young man:

Kali was of average height, well-proportioned and strong-limbed, and had light chestnut hair. He was very popular, and a man of more than average ability. He made this verse:

At nine skills I challenge -
a champion at chess:
runes I rarely spoil,
I read books and write:
I'm skilled at skiing
and shooting and sculling
and more! - I've mastered music and verse.

Maybe modesty wasn't Kali's greatest spiritual attribute. Nevertheless, he always seemed to be an engaging and popular character.

Kali was very popular among the young men in the taverns of

Bergen. He was often called upon to mediate in disputes, and after one such occasion, King Sigurd granted Kali half of Orkney, and gave him the title of earl. He took the name Rognvald.

It was one thing to be called Earl of Orkney, it was another to claim the title. He made one attempt, but had to retreat. At his father's suggestion, he made a solemn vow that if he won the earldom, he would build a magnificent stone minster in Kirkwall. When he became earl, he appointed his father, Kol, to supervise the building project.

Rognvald had another ambition - to be a pilgrim. So he set off with Bishop William the Old and some friends for Jerusalem. At Narbonne, he chatted up the beautiful Queen Ermingerd, but he was determined to complete the pilgrimage.

They all went and bathed in the River Jordan and, with Sigmund Fish-Hook, Earl Rognvald swam across the river. After that they went back to Jerusalem, and the Earl made this verse as they approached the city:

> *A cross on this bard's*
> *breast, on his back*
> *a palm-branch: peacefully*
> *we pace the hillside.*

There's something very touchingly innocent and child-like about these men from Orkney splashing about in the River Jordan, and Earl Rognvald, along with his pal Sigmund Fish-Hook, swimming across the river as if it were the inter-island games.

After many adventures, the men eventually returned to Orkney, where Earl Rognvald was given a great welcome. There were continual battles and skirmishes, but Rognvald ruled Orkney for 22 years. He met his death in an ambush in Caithness. His relics were eventually translated to St Magnus Cathedral.

Was he a saint? Not in conventional terms. But sometimes conventional terms are misleading. A saint is not a perfect person. A saint may be someone who loves life, who loves God, and, who, despite his imperfections, points us to God. Rognvald teaches us that it takes all kinds to make a saint, all kinds to make a church.

WHY ST MAGNUS CATHEDRAL WAS BUILT, AND HOW IT CHANGED

Bryce Wilson

St Magnus Cathedral has survived religious and political change and the ravages of time. Wind, water and fire have taken their toll, and sinking foundations have threatened its very existence. This book traces the changes and events in the life of the building, which stands as a monument to the many generations entrusted with its care. It also highlights the less obvious aspects of the Cathedral that give it its unique character.

Earl's Palace and Cathedral, painted by J. Spottiswoode in 1802 (courtesy of Lady Elizabeth Temple).

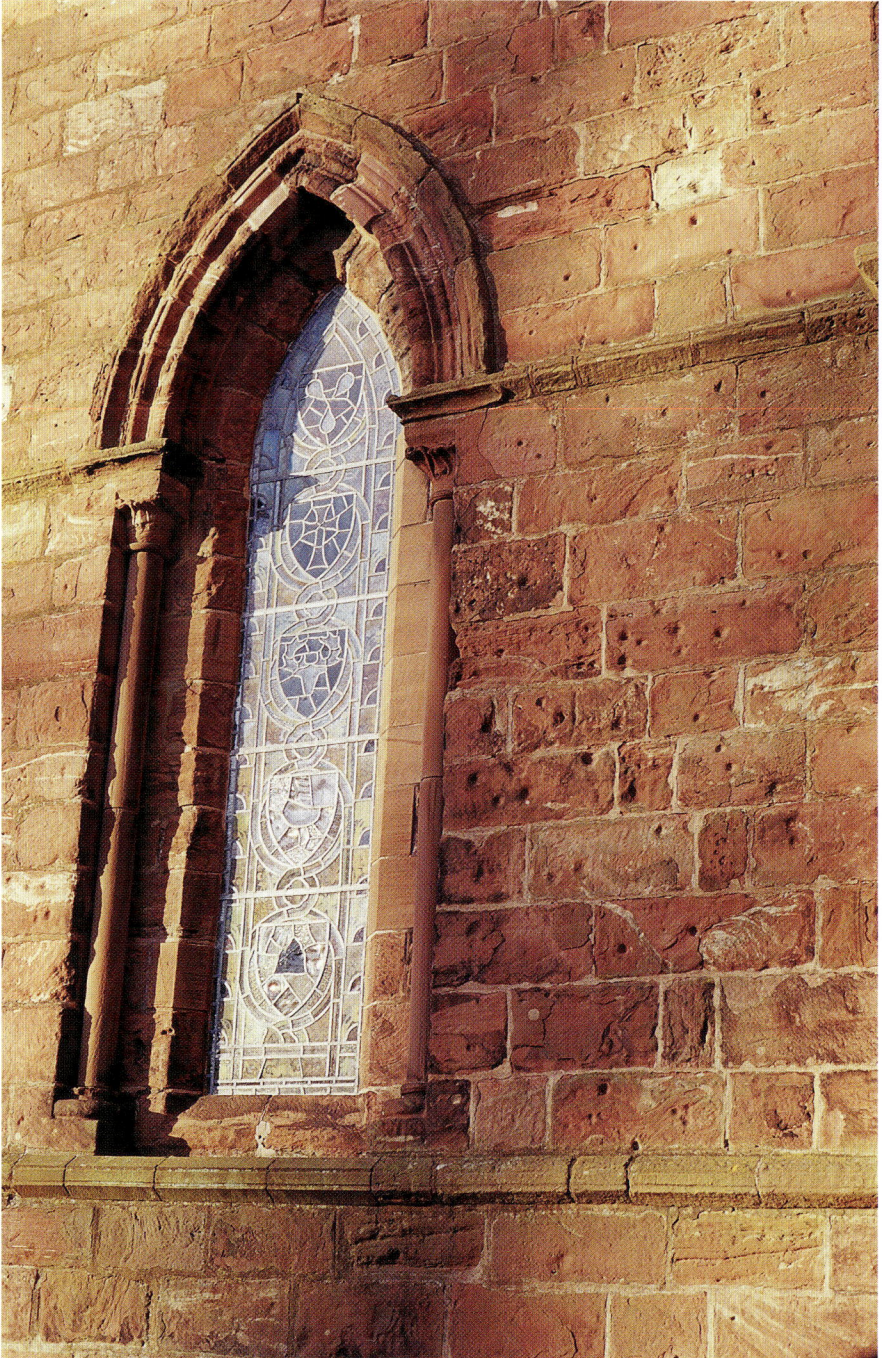

Musket ball marks on the east side of the south transept.

It was as a bishop's seat and a place of pilgrimage that the Cathedral began its life, more than eight centuries ago. The founder, Earl Rognvald Kolsson, dried the sails of his longship in the nave. Much later, Cromwell's troops were billeted there. Witches were tried by church courts and sentenced to be worried at the stake; during Robert Stewart's hapless rebellion, muskets were fired from the bell tower. Today, the Cathedral houses a congregation of the Church of Scotland, is a favoured venue for musical performances, and is greatly admired as a rare and outstanding survival of medieval church architecture.

Hangman's ladder in the triforium.

Why the Cathedral was built

The Vikings who invaded Orkney centuries before the Cathedral was built had given way to farmers and merchants. By the 12th century Orkney was the centre of a powerful Norse earldom which had gradually adopted the Christian religion and European culture. For the earl and the bishop, a cathedral was a fitting symbol of power and status. Christian beliefs were deeply held. People thought that the relics of saints - usually their bones - could assist their own prayers, bring about cures and other miracles and aid them on their way to heaven. Pilgrims were prepared to make long journeys to pray in the church in which the saint's relics were housed. They would then give money to that church.

The bones of St Magnus.

The Cult of Saint Magnus.

The Bishop of Orkney had only a small cathedral church - Christ's Church in Birsay - believed to be on the site now occupied by the parish church of St Magnus. In the early 12th century the Orkney earldom was divided between two Norse earls - Magnus Erlendsson and his cousin Hakon. About the year 1116, a struggle for power led to the murder of Magnus by Hakon, on the island of Egilsay.

Magnus Erlendsson was a pious man, and considered to be a martyr. He was buried in Christ's Church in Birsay, and soon there were stories of miraculous cures associated with his burial place. The Bishop of Orkney bowed to public opinion and declared Magnus a saint (as bishops at that time were allowed to do).

The cult of St Magnus spread far and wide. Churches were dedicated to his name in Faroe, Iceland and London, and his figure appears on Scandinavian altarpieces. Hymns dedicated to St Magnus have survived in Gaelic and Latin.

Mould for crosses cast in lead and sold to medieval pilgrims to the shrine of St Magnus (The Orkney Museum).

St Magnus on the altarpiece from Andenes, Norway (Courtesy of the University of Tromsø).

A major building project.

Twenty years after the death of Magnus Erlendsson, his nephew Rognvald Kolsson came from Norway to overthrow Hakon's son Paul and become Earl of Orkney. By encouraging the veneration of the bones of his uncle, St. Magnus, he knew he could only strengthen his position as earl. Rognvald would probably have seen the Cathedral of St. Swithin in Stavangar, which was nearing completion. He made a vow that if he succeeded in regaining the earldom he would built a magnificent stone church in Kirkwall to contain the bones of St. Magnus, and would endow it with estates for its upkeep. This he now proceeded to do, and the work began in 1137.

St Magnus Hymn, *Nobilis humilis*, 13th century (Courtesy of Uppsala University).

Rognvald's father Kol, a chieftain from Norway, directed the building work, employing masons who had recently worked on Durham Cathedral. There was great activity. Quarries were opened at the Head of Holland and on the island of Eday. The stone was landed by boats on the shore of the Peerie Sea , which then reached what is now Broad Street. (Excavations under Tankerness House in the 1970s revealed a jetty and fragments of red sandstone.)

This was a major building project, and within a few short years Rognvald ran out of money. He solved this by suggesting a single payment from Orkney farmers, based on the size of their farms. They in return would receive freehold rights to their property. The farmers were well pleased with this arrangement, made payment, and the work continued.

The original design (the facade towers were never built).

The building was closely modelled on Durham Cathedral, and it looked very different from the way it does today. The internal walls, ceilings and pillars were plastered and painted with colourful floral patterns (fragments of which survive). It was dramatically situated close to the shore of the Peerie Sea, harbour of the Norse longships.

The Cathedral's main purpose was to house the relics - the bones - of St. Magnus. This would attract pilgrims, and income, from distant places. By 1152 the choir and three pillars of the nave had been built, and a temporary west front had been erected. (Twin towers were planned for the west front. Started but never built, their foundations were discovered by workmen in the early 20th century).

A surviving fragment of medieval floral decoration in the nave.

The Cardinal, by Stanley Cursiter R.S.A., P.R.S.W. One of a series of paintings
displayed in the Supper Room of Kirkwall Town Hall.

A semicircular area called the apse was built at the east end, behind the high altar. Here the bones were hidden in a casket called a reliquary, itself contained within a large, highly ornamented shrine. As pilgrims' gifts of money gathered, some of this wealth would have been lavished in gold work and precious stones.

Pilgrims approached the Saint's reliquary with a great sense of awe. They would have been preparing throughout a long journey for the moment of admission to the Saint's presence. When they entered the church they first had to walk the length of the nave and pass beneath the tower; they then approached the shrine along one side aisle, and left it by the other. The nearer the shrine they approached, the greater the feeling of reverence. By the end of the 12th century two chapels had been added to the transepts of the Cathedral.

The box in which the bones of St Magnus were discovered in 1919 (The Orkney Museum).

Gateway of Tankerness House, formerly Sub-chantry, Archdeanery and Chancellory of the Cathedral.

Growth of the Cathedral

The Cathedral continued to change and grow over the next two centuries. The services held in cathedrals became more elaborate. More and more music was used, and space had to be found for choristers as well as for an increasing number of priests, deacons and lesser officials, all of whom wanted their own seats in the east end of the church.

St Magnus Cathedral underwent major changes. The apse was pulled down, and the choir extended by the presbytery. The relics of St Magnus would have been moved to a less central but still prominent position. Plans were made to extend the nave. Work was started on a new facade, but it would stand unfinished for two centuries, when it was completed by Bishop Thomas Tulloch.

In 1544 the powerful Bishop Reid raised a formidable band of

Remains of the Bishop's Palace, rebuilt by Robert Reid in the 16th century (drawn by R. W. Billings).

Carving from the medieval choir stalls (loaned to The Orkney Museum by The National Museums of Scotland).

clerics to ensure the efficient administration of the Cathedral and its activities. They were accommodated across Broad Street in a row of manses on land reclaimed from the Peerie Sea. Where the Town Hall now stands was the Provostrie, followed southwards by the Treasury (on the site now occupied by Judith Glue). Then came the Sub-chantry, the Arch-deanery and the Chancellory.

The west facade.   (Photo © Gunni Moberg)

(After the reformation of 1560 Gilbert Foulzie, the Cathedral's last priest and first minister, acquired the Sub-chantry and the Arch-deanery, now known as Tankerness House - his initials are carved above the gateway); the adjoining Chancellory at the top of Tankerness Lane became part of the same house in the late 18th century. Across the way stands Reid's original Grammar School. He also rebuilt the Bishop's Palace and added the Moosie Tooer.

On the right is the Provostrie, where the Town Hall now stands.

Famine and plague affect the Cathedral

Changes in the climate and the spread of disease in the 14th century made people believe that they had incurred the wrath of God. Europe was becoming cooler and wetter. Crops failed, and many people died of starvation.

The Black Death, a fearsome plague which spread from the east, left one-third of Europe's population dead, and it kept coming back. The plague was interpreted as God's anger at the sinfulness of the age. After death was the fearful prospect of Hell or Purgatory, for God's anger made it very difficult to get to Heaven. People became obsessed with death.

The wealthy and powerful arranged to be buried in churches and cathedrals under elaborate tombs. They paid priests to say prayers before the tombs, believing that this would shorten the time the soul had to spend in Purgatory, before its release to join the Saints in Heaven.

Inscribed lead plate and bone handle from the tomb of Bishop William the Old. "Here lies William the Old of happy memory, the first bishop" (loaned to The Orkney Museum by the National Museums of Scotland).

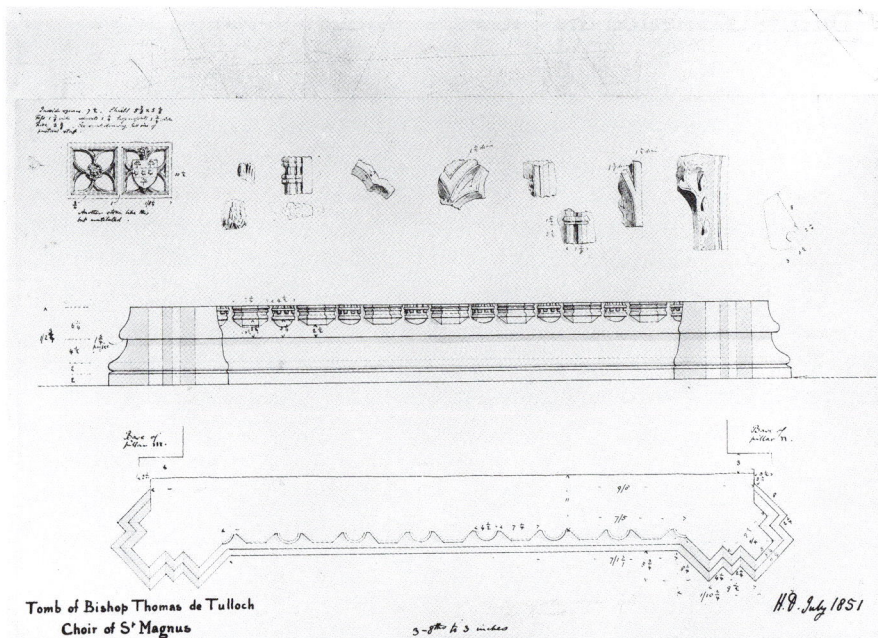

Tomb of Bishop Thomas de Tulloch
Choir of St Magnus

H.D. *July 1851*

Drawing of the remains of Bishop Thomas Tulloch's tomb by Sir Henry Dryden.

Oak crozier head and wax replicas of chalice and paten from the grave of Bishop
Thomas Tulloch (loaned to The Orkney Museum by The National Museums of
Scotland).

During this period the Cathedral would have contained several elaborate bishops' tombs. The surviving remains show that Bishop Thomas Tulloch had one of the most splendid canopied tombs in Scotland. It stood between the easternmost piers of the choir arcade, facing into the south aisle. It became famous as the place in Kirkwall where business contracts and debts were settled - an agreement made at the Bishop's tomb was considered as binding as a legal contract.

Thomas Tulloch's tomb survived until the 17th century, when Oliver Cromwell's troops were garrisoned in the Cathedral. They are said to have stolen the tomb's copper canopy, and left only the broken base standing. (It is now preserved in The Orkney Museum.)

The Earl's seat (formerly the Bishop's) and the Graham Gallery before they were removed in the 19th century.

The Reformation brings more changes.

The Reformation of the Church in Scotland in 1560 brought desecration and ruin to many cathedrals. St Magnus Cathedral was unique in that for more than seventy years it had through the decree of King James III of Scotland belonged to the Royal Burgh of Kirkwall. It now survived to become the Parish Church of Kirkwall. No longer was it a place of pilgrimage to the shrine of Saint Magnus, whose bones were placed in a plain wooden box and buried in a pillar (where they were found in 1919). The organ, treasures and rich vestments were removed, and the wall decorations were covered in whitewash.

Services were now held in the choir and presbytery, where important families and trade guilds were allowed to set up their

Remains of the Earl's Seat stored in the triforium.

Panels removed from the Cathedral in the mid-19th century (The Orkney Museum).

Arms of Kirkwall from the Sailor's Loft.

Gravestone of the merchant Patrick Prince, who died in 1673.

Gravestone of Elizabeth Cuthbert, who died in 1685. Her husband James Wallace was minister of the Cathedral.

own pews and galleries. Bishop George Graham built a gallery for his family, and earl Robert Stewart himself had a seat (believed to have formerly been that of the Catholic bishop). The nave, no longer used for worship, was reserved as a burial place for leading families.

The 17th century Mort Brod in the north aisle of the nave. A memorial for Robert Nicolson, glazier, it was almost certainly the work of his son James who painted the face of the Cathedral clock and two sundials.

One of two 17th century Dutch collection plates portraying the Garden of Eden.

Lightning destroys the spire

It is recorded that the Cathedral originally had 'a lofty spire' made of wood and probably covered in lead. In 1671 the spire was struck by lightning and caught fire "to the great astonishment and terrification of the beholders". The bells fell to the ground where they were saved by a hastily garnered heap of earth. The spire was replaced some years later by the low, slate-covered pyramid which survived until the early 20th century.

The large bell temporarily removed in the early 20th century.

The Government intervenes.

In 1845 the Government assumed ownership, expelled the congregation and carried out restoration of the Cathedral as an historic monument. In the process the bishop's and earl's seats were removed. They also uncovered the bones of the first bishop of St Magnus Cathedral, William the Old, and those of Bishop Thomas Tulloch. In 1851 the Royal Burgh of Kirkwall re-established ownership of the building. Choir and presbytery were fitted with new pews and galleries for the reinstated congregation, and a glazed screen was erected to separate the choir from the nave.

Silver cross found in a grave in the 1840s (loaned to The Orkney Museum by The National Museums of Scotland).

THE CHOIR, ST.MAGNUS CATHEDRAL, KIRKWALL. TK.

Pews and galleries installed in choir and presbytery in the 1850s. The glass screen separated choir from nave.

Gallery in the north aisle of the choir and presbytery.

One of Sir Henry Dryden's Cathedral sketchbooks. He carried out detailed studies of the building in the mid-19th century (The Orkney Museum).

Major restoration.

The building remained internally divided and slowly deteriorating until the early 20th century, when the Thoms Bequest made major restoration possible. Three architects submitted competitive plans. One scheme provided for all the wooden doors to be replaced with bronze, cast with Biblical scenes. A soaring pulpit was envisaged, and mural paintings mounted in the triforium arches. Public unease at the danger of over-restoring an already superb building may have led the Council to proceed on the less elaborate but still extensive scheme submitted by the Edinburgh architect George Mackie Watson.

On the left is the wooden belfry used during the restoration.
Stanley Cursiter R.S.A., P.R.S.W., 1914.

The nave under restoration.   Stanley Cursiter R.S.A., P.R.S.W., 1914.

The only major external change was the tall steeple, replacing the low pyramid roof of the bell tower. Within, the screen separating the choir from the nave was removed, along with the pews and galleries. However, the long vista of nave and choir was again lost by the positioning of the organ screen. The formerly plain windows now boasted stained glass, much of the floor was tiled, and the warm red sandstone of the interior was exposed by removing plaster and whitewash. By 1930 the work was complete.

In the 1960s the Saint Rognvald Chapel was arranged in the east end. Wood carvings of Kol, Magnus and Rognvald look down on lectern and table, incorporating some of the fine 17th century carved wood panels which had been removed a century before. Soon, however, it was realized that the building was in serious crisis. Sinking foundations meant that the nave was gradually leaning westward, the gable in danger of collapsing into Broad Street. An Appeal Committee raised £300,000 and by 1974 a network of steel girders, concealed above the nave and clerestory ceilings, ensured the survival of the building.

The Lammas Fair.   Stanley Cursiter R.S.A., P.R.S.W., 1914.

Removing the low spire.

All this while, erosion of the carved stonework on the exterior of the building was causing serious concern. In 1982 a proposal was made to protect the west facade from further deterioration by adding a porch. The scheme was abandoned in the face of a public protest that it would ruin the aspect of the west facade "which is, in itself, acclaimed internationally as a marvellous example of the finest period of church building....there is no reason why the eroded stonework over the west doors cannot be replaced, gradually, by local masons, trained for the purpose".

Much work has been carried out over the past century, bringing the maintenance of the Cathedral to a high standard. For the most part good sense has prevailed, and it has escaped over-restoration. Skilled masons are now permanently employed, and the original stonework is wherever possible retained.

Designs for bronze doors, a soaring pulpit and Biblical scenes were abandoned.

Plan of Pinnacle

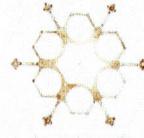

Plan above Sounding Board

Soffit of Canopy

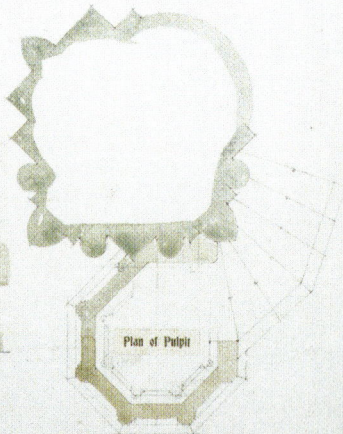

Plan of Pulpit

Elevation of Pulpit

Proposed Decoration for Triforium Openings

St Magnus. The stained glass windows were installed under the Thoms Bequest.

THE STONE CARVINGS

Tom Muir

St. Magnus Cathedral is greatly enhanced by its wealth of carved stone ornamentation. This is to be found both inside and outside the building, and is often overlooked, but it tells us a lot about the Church at the time, and the people who worked for it. The masons who fashioned the building are recorded by the mason's marks that are to be found on the carved stone. These marks were not merely a testimony of the worker's skill, but ensured that he had completed his task to the required standard.

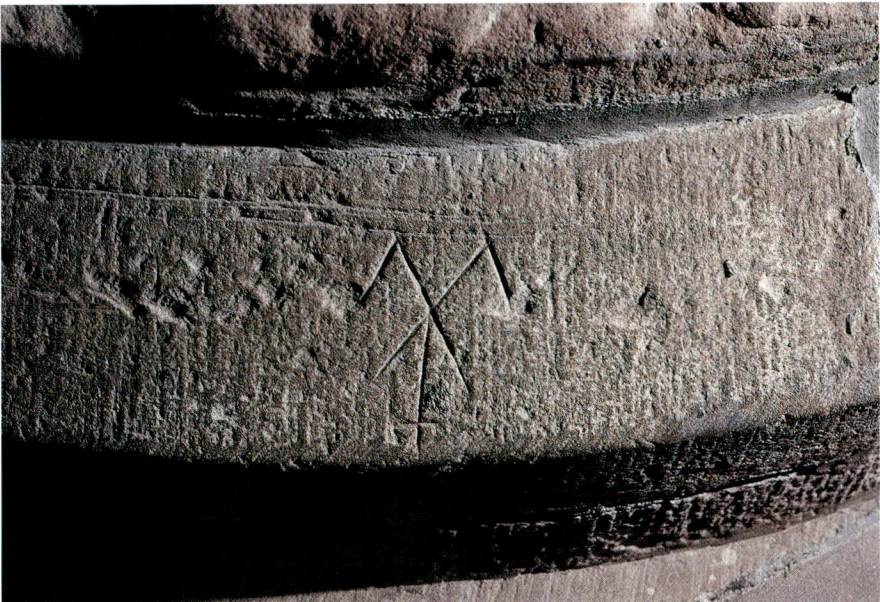

Mason's mark in the nave.

Two heads in the NE side of nave.

Stylized animal heads in the presbytery.

Stylized human heads in the SE side of the nave.

Knights Templar cross in the south transept.

   On the north side of the nave there is a series of carved human heads at the base of the roof supports. They are depicted in pairs, and are natural looking. One of these heads has its hand in front of its mouth, as though it had just said something it shouldn't have. The south side has mostly pillars built into the wall as supports, but the carvings that have survived are stylized human and animal heads. Above the triforium (upper floor) there are carved dragon heads. On the west wall of the south transept there is carved a cross in the style of the Knights Templar. This equal-armed cross was the symbol used in the medieval crusades to the Holy Land. Two other crosses are to be found high up in the straight-fronted pillars of the choir. They are modern, and mark the resting places of St Magnus (south pillar) and St Rognvald (north pillar).

Burial place of St Magnus, south of organ screen.

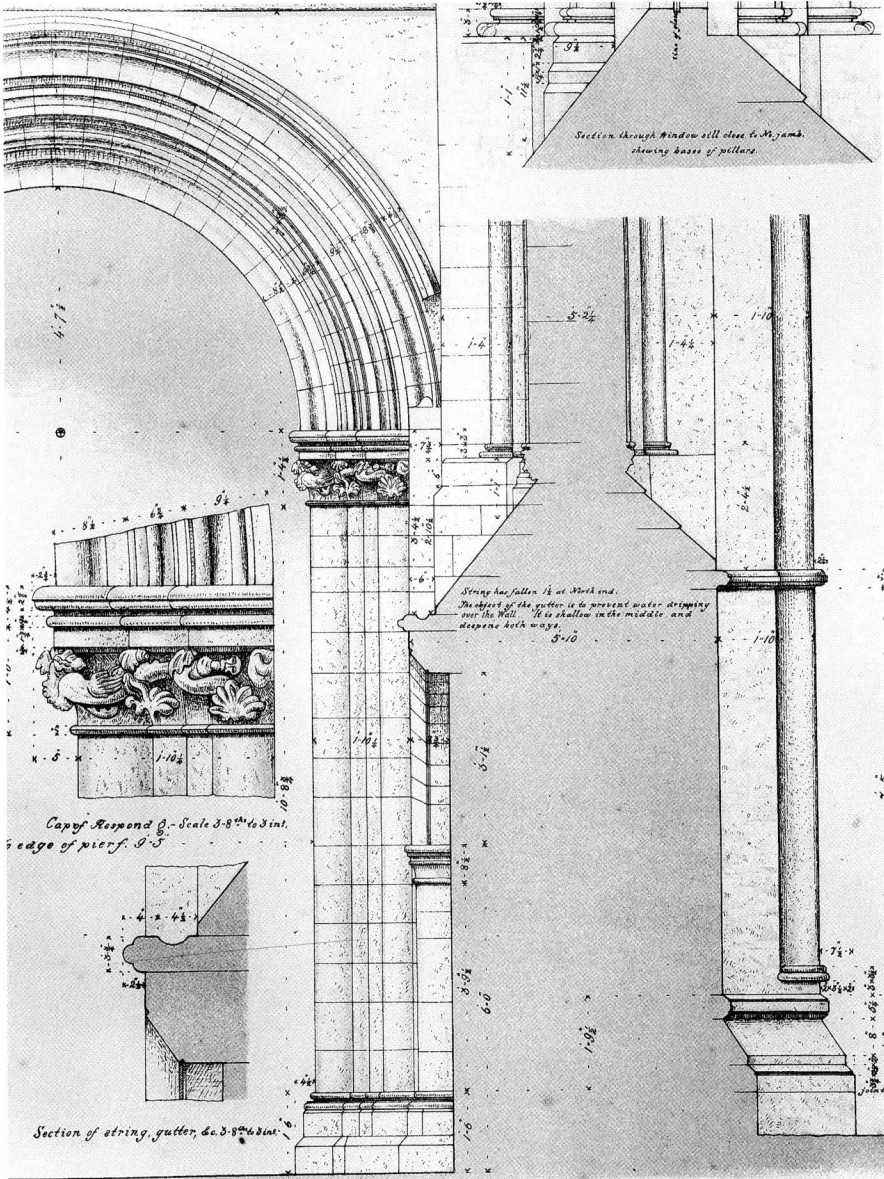

Drawing of the choir by Sir Henry Dryden in 1845.

Drawing of the choir by Sir Henry Dryden in 1845.

In the early 13th century the east end of the Cathedral was demolished and the building extended. Here we see a departure from the Romanesque style of building tradition, epitomized by its round-topped arches, and a move towards the then fashionable Gothic style, with its pointed arch windows. While the windows are of Gothic design, the arches of the pillars are still fashioned in the Romanesque style. The pillars themselves are more elaborate than the plain round ones of the nave, and have most of the finest carvings. The capitals of the pillars are decorated with foliage, amongst which can be seen grotesque human heads. To the north side of the rose window there are two dragons facing one another. It is difficult to say what the influences were for this carving, as dragons are to be found in cathedral carvings in both Norway and Scotland.

Hooded figure on SE pillar in the presbytery.

Green Men on SE pillar in the presbytery.

Grotesque human heads on NW pillar in the presbytery.

Dragons on north side of the rose window.

Sheela-na-Gig on SW pillar of presbytery.

On the south-east pillar there is a carving of a small human figure wearing a hood. On the other side of the same pillar there are two Green Men, and two human-like figures with lizard-like bodies. There is another Green Man on the north wall of the presbytery, with foliage growing out of his mouth. These symbols of human heads, covered with or sprouting foliage from their mouths, were used in churches of this period, having been influenced by ancient Roman carvings. They were originally fertility symbols, used by the Church to represent the corruption of the flesh; leaves were often used to represent decay and sin. The faces of the Green Men were depicted as being grotesque, while their Roman counterparts were usually benevolent looking.

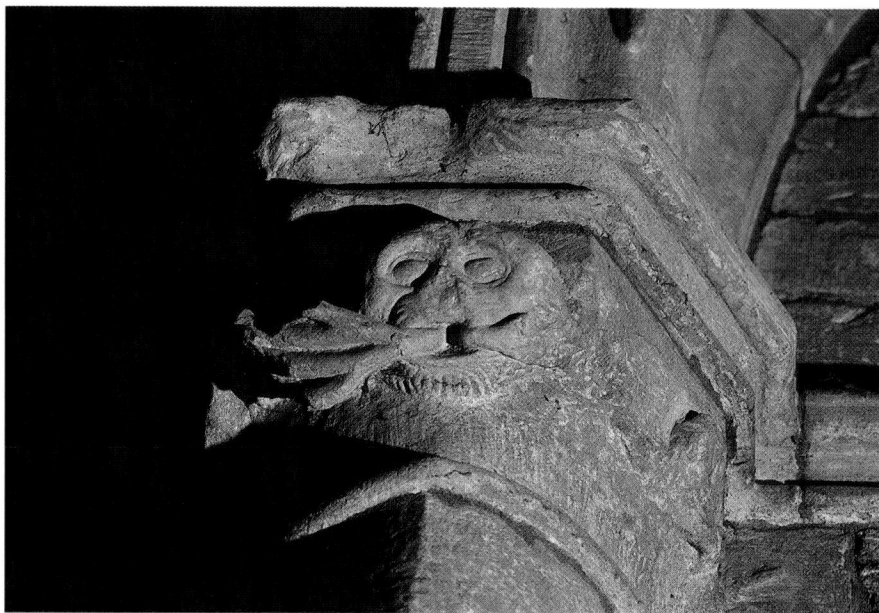

Single Green Man on north presbytery wall.

Statue of St Magnus, from the 14th century.

On the south-west pillar of the presbytery is a small carving of a Sheela-na-Gig. This represents a squatting female figure with open legs, displaying her genitals. They look grotesque, and represent sinfulness and lust. The Sheela-na-Gig dates back to the 11th century, when it was used on churches in France. From there it spread to northern Spain, England and Ireland. It became a popular image in Irish churches, and was also used to decorate secular buildings, such as castles. The name Sheela-na-Gig is Irish, meaning a woman of ill repute. It is relatively scarce in Scotland.

Outside the building there are gargoyles looking out from the walls, and around the tower. These were put there in the early 20th century during restoration, as were the rows of human heads around the tower. There are many carvings to be seen, including a head with three faces on the east end above the rose window. The front of the Cathedral has plinths originally intended to support statues of the saints. They were probably destroyed during the Reformation, or in the mid 17th century when Cromwell's troops were billeted in the Cathedral. The pillars next to the main west door are hollow, originally intended to be carved into, but never completed.

Two carved images of St Magnus and St Olaf were discovered in the Cathedral, and are now on display in The Orkney Museum. The figure of St Magnus dates from the early 14th century, while that of St Olaf is early 15th century. The figure of St Magnus shows him as a beardless man holding a sword to symbolize his martyrdom, while his other hand clutches his cloak-string. Around his head is a ribbon, representing his status as an earl. The German title 'hertug' (meaning duke) was introduced into Norway in 1237 by King Hakon. The badge of office was a ribbon, sometimes decorated with flowers, which was worn around the head. Although Magnus was an earl, and the title of duke had not been introduced at the time of his death, he is depicted in this carving wearing the ribbon around his head, to show that he was a man of importance.

Statue of St Olaf, from the 15th century.

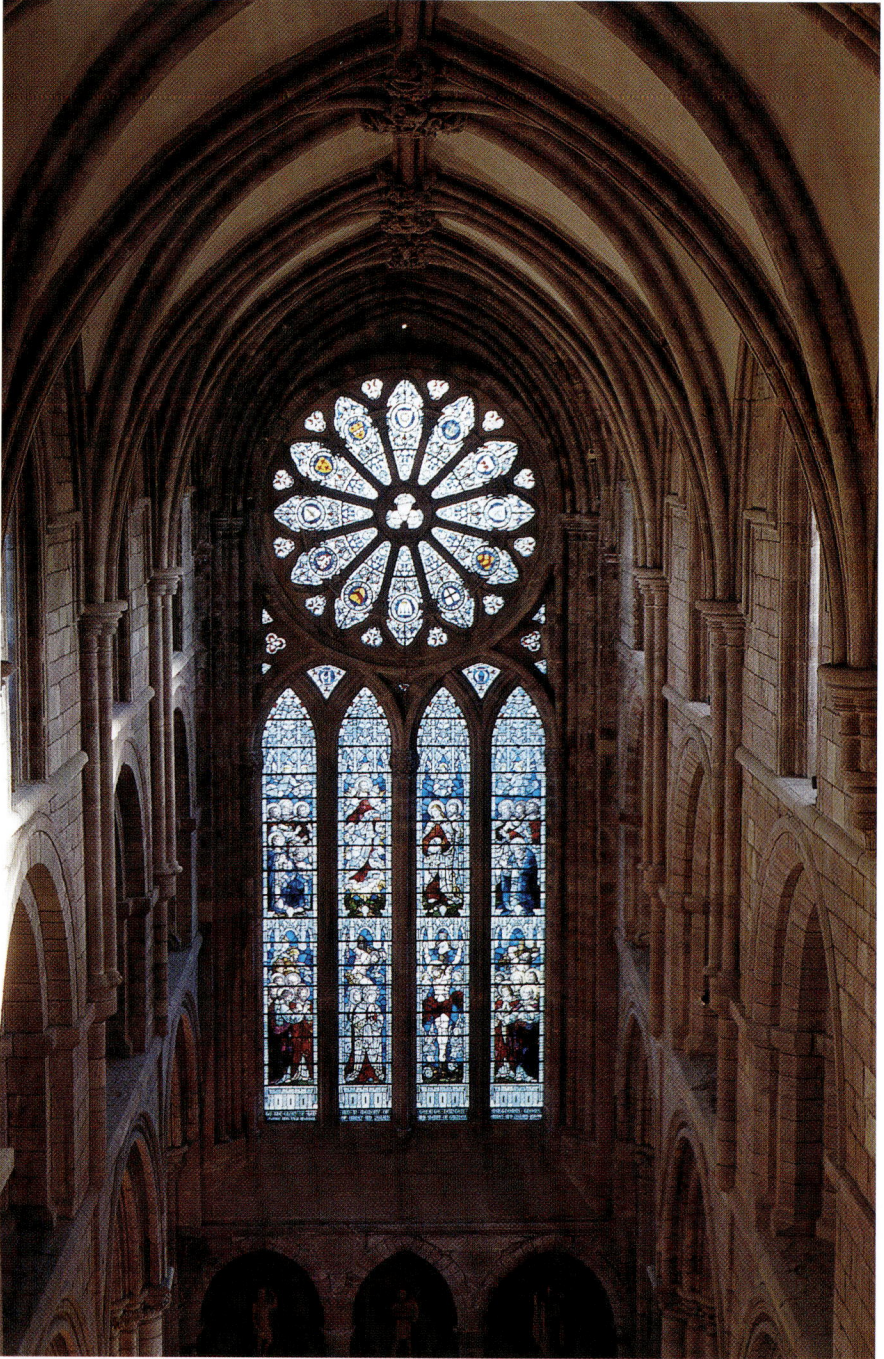

The rose window, dedicated to George Hunter Thoms.

BELL-RINGERS AND CARETAKERS, KIRK AND COUNCIL:
a brief history of a sometimes fraught situation...

Jim Rousay

Nothing is know of any person responsible for the running of the basics of the building prior to the mid 17th century, when apparently a character called Cowper may have resided in the Cathedral, possibly in or below the bell chamber. This speculation, cited by Buckham Hugh Hossack in *Kirkwall in the Orkneys*, is dependent on there being a floor below the belfry in those days. At that time the bells would have seen more secular use, thought the post of bell-ringer would have been a Kirk Session appointment, thus one Harry Grott from 1660-73 and James Laughton from 1673 onwards. Hossack also refers to the role of the Beadle in keeping order, and cites an argument over the key to the Sinclairs' Loft, the Kirk Session desiring that this be kept by the Beadle, along with the other keys, which would seem to suggest that the Kirk ran the building. However, there are references to "barbarous practices" of the Town Guard in the building, and a few accounts of wars over seating and pews, indicating that the Kirk of those days did not have full control of the use of the building. John Mooney in *The Cathedral and Royal Burgh of Kirkwall* cites a reference to the appointment of a Bellman/Beadle, c. 1636, and the need for this person to stay in town, the previous appointee apparently not being available when required, which indicates again a combining of roles.

There are few references to the situation in the 18th century, but it is only during the 1820s that the references to personnel and to the building begin to burgeon. The Kirk Session Minutes of 29th March 1831 refer to a petition from one James Fotheringhame, Bellman, asking to be paid "for ringing the bells and airing the Church at the old rates", the Session agreeing to his request. The use of the term "Bellman" here is probably not to be confused with the Town Council office of "Common Crier and Bellman", a post lost and regained by one James Wallace in late 1826. Mr Wallace, refused spirits by the proprietress of a town inn, used

The nave, looking to the rose window.

the Bell to publicly attack the reputation of the lady and lost his post, but was reinstated via a petition, a fine, and a cut in wages, "the Council being always the only judges with respect to his conduct".

Back in the Cathedral, October 1831 saw work begin on a new gallery in the west end of the choir, and by December, there was another argument over seating, with Mr Fotheringhame, the Bellman-Beadle, agreeing, eventually, to share his seat with one Mr Heddle. The seating, or accommodation problem, from the perspective of the Kirk Session, was coming to a head. In early 1832, a representation was made to the Heritors of the Cathedral "respecting the grievances so justly complained of from the want of proper accommodation in Saint Magnus Church...". The Kirk Session then resolved to consult with the Church Procurator, since their representation had been refused by one of the principal heritors, perhaps an early shot in a battle for control of the building which was to gain momentum as the value of the inheritance was realised by the Heritors. However, there was a certain amount of give and take in appointments: the death of the Second Minister, the Reverend Mr Gunn, in late 1830, sees the Town Council discussing a replacement in January 1831, with a special meeting to be held and the Congregation consulted. Later that month, a petition from the Congregation is read, stating that the successor to the Reverend Gunn be "agreeable to and recommended by" them. It would seem that the Town Council had a right of patronage in the appointment of major Kirk officials, and that the Kirk was left to appoint the minor figures as it saw fit, and the running of the building was very much the province of the Kirk Session.

Thus in November 1833, the Kirk Session is concerned over irregularities in the keeping of the clock, these being occasioned by gales of wind moving the hands and concludes "that it is desirable to have a stated day in the week for winding up and regulating the clock to the true time, and resolve that the Keeper of the Clock shall wind up and regulate it only in the Friday of each week at or before noon, and that he shall regulate by the sun when possible or when otherwise by the Time Piece in the choir". Here, obviously, the Clock and Bells have their respective appointees, both chosen by the Kirk Session, for in October 1837, the Kirk Session appoints "James Elrick, Watchmaker", as Keeper of the Clock, though in September 1839, when the clock is to be refurbished, the Session consults the Town Council, who pay two thirds of the costs. The estimate and nature of the repairs and refurbishment was prepared by James Elrick, but that did not prevent the Session, in November 1839, from resolving that:

"both the public clocks in the Church have been kept irregularly of late, by which much dissatisfaction has been given to the public..."

The Kirk Session then undertook to remind Mr Elrick to attend to his duties or another Keeper would be appointed.

The period 1840-1851 saw the Kirk and Town Council locked in combat with the Government Office of Woods and Forests over the right to and the use of the Cathedral, resulting in a victory for Kirk and Council, who regained possession of a building now made wind-and water-tight by the Crown. Little can be gleaned of the activities of the beadles and bellmen of this period, so the system of Kirk appointees must have continued. In August 1878, a note of dissatisfaction is (literally) heard:

"It was remitted to the Works Committee to make the necessary

Clock made by Hugh Gordon, Aberdeen, in 1761. It was replaced in the early 20th century.

management with the person in charge of the Cathedral Bells to secure their proper use and harmony during the Lammas Fair, and to prevent boys and others ringing them indiscriminately at all times."

Following this in the Minute is the first municipal appointment to a minor post in the Cathedral and a sign that the heritors of the building are taking more control of it:

"It was unanimously agreed to authorise the treasurer to pay Mr Peter Guthrie a salary at the rate of three pounds three shillings per annum for ringing the evening or eight o'clock bell commencing as at 15th April last and on the understanding that he will also ring the bell for the usual time at five minutes to ten o'clock on the morning of every weekday in time to come."

Kirkwall Town Council, representing, in the main, the Heritors, was by now fully aware of the value of the Cathedral and took steps to ensure that it be protected from structural damage and vandalism. Part of the remit of the successor to Peter Guthrie, who died in 1891, concerns not only the ringing of the curfew bell but also:

"as to the charge of admission to strangers and others to the cathedral, and as to the preservation of the building and prevention of carving or scratching of names or initials thereon, and taking measures to that effect."

Consequently, on August 14th 1892, Mr Peter Wick was officially given the job of ringing the curfew bell and looking after the building, though there is no naming of his position. His duties were as follows:

"that he attend to the keeping of that part of the cathedral under the control of the Town Council...that he be instructed to prevent the cutting or carving of initials on any part of the cathedral..."

Strangers were to be charged sixpence each and threepence when there were more than one, and residents got in free. Printed notices of the admission charges and the prohibition on defacing the building were to be displayed on the doors of the building. The Town Council did not wish to change the existing Lammas Fair arrangement, when everyone paid one penny admission charge.

If the Town Council was being careful not to "interfere with the right of the public" in regard to admission during the Lammas

Peter Wick, Bell-ringer and Caretaker, 1892 - 1902.

Fair, this same meeting saw public right defended further, and at the expense of the Kirk Session, which had apparently overreached itself. The Council, largely due to the highlighting of the issue by Baillie Nicol Spence, was...

"...to take steps to ensure the rights of the public to a small room in the cathedral, presently occupied by the established church and the clerk was instructed to write the Session Clerk of the Congregation worshipping in the Cathedral requesting to be informed upon what authority said room has been taken possession of and occupied by said congregation without permission asked and obtained from the Council".

Further friction with the Kirk Session came when the successor to the late Peter Wick was sought, in early 1902. There were three applicants for the post, still untitled, the successful applicant being one William Williamson, a watchmaker and a temporary bell-ringer, who probably looked after the clock and helped Peter Wick. The conditions were as in 1892, though with extra emphasis placed on keeping "regularly and constantly clean that part of the cathedral under the control and jurisdiction of the Council." However, the Session Clerk was not pleased by this appointment, and reminded the Council, by letter, that since the Kirk Session pay one pound per year towards the cost of ringing the eight o'clock bell, they expect to be consulted in the choice of applicant. This stance is rebutted by the Council, resulting in another letter from the Session Clerk reminding them that the Kirk Session had organized the ringing of the bell for the past fifty years...

In April 1903 Councillor Hewison gave notice that at the next monthly meeting he would call attention to the inadequacy of the remuneration paid to the Caretaker of St Magnus Cathedral. This is the first reference to a job title for the situation, and employees were apparently able to lobby councillors in those days. Alas, come the May meeting, Councillor Hewison decided not to proceed with his motion, as Councillor Reid intended to propose an increase in the present charge of admission to the building of strangers, when there are more than one, from threepence to sixpence. Does this indicate that the wages of the Caretaker (first reference to this title) were coming partly from sources other than the Town Council? The answer probably lies in the nature of duties inherited, such as bell-ringing, for which a contribution from the Kirk might have been expected, and the charge levied on visitors, from which the Caretaker may have received a cut. Nevertheless, there does appear to be a reluctance on the part of the Town Council to foot the full wages bill of the now Caretaker, probably as a result of the stance taken by the Kirk, namely that they should be involved in the appointment process.

In April 1908, Mr Williamson, still being Caretaker, wrote to Provost Slater, expressing his concern over broken chains on the roof hatches, a roof door requiring a new hinge, and several broken window panes, his report being approved of. This is an early example of the relationship of the Cathedral Caretakers with the Town Council itself, and shows that the Caretakers were Council men, as opposed to being appointees of the Kirk Session.

By this time the Sheriff Thoms Bequest was a reality and in August 1909 the Town Council decided to set up a management committee for the running of their building. This Committee of six was equally composed of Council and Kirk appointees, and would have an election on the November of each year. There were four main aims:

"1. To make regulations as to the admission of visitors to the Cathedral on weekdays, except on occasions when services are to be held therein.

2. To appoint the requisite officials for and to regulate the cleaning, lighting and heating of the Cathedral.

3. To apply to the cleaning, lighting and heating and upkeep of the internal fittings any monies derived from the admission of visitors or otherwise.

4. To control the ringing of the bells and to take charge of the clock."

This Town Council Cathedral Committee, as it came to be called, was probably just what the building required : a single body through which all matters pertaining to the care and running of the building had to be submitted, and Mr Williamson was not aback in doing so and taking responsibility for his actions, though it is interesting to note that the following report is given to Provost Slater in the first instance...

"Provost Slater reported that Mr Williamson, the Bell-ringer of St Magnus Cathedral had informed him that the tongue of the curfew bell fell last night and that the bells would need to be examined as to their safety; and that he had instructed the Bell-ringer to get Mr Leslie, Blacksmith, to examine the bells."

The choir and presbytery, now the St Rognvald Chapel.

The years prior to and including the First World War saw the complete refurbishment of the building as the Town Council's most prized possession and as a place of worship, and by December 1917, the Provost could state that the restored portion of the Cathedral was to be opened on Christmas Day at noon. The Council resolved to attend the service to be then held.

Did peace and love and good management then prevail in this wonderfully rehabilitated building? Maybe not, for in December 1927, we have Councillor Garrioch asking that a committee be appointed to enquire into the question of who has the power of appointment of a Caretaker to the Cathedral. By January 1928, this Committee decided, after considering the matter "that the Appointment of a Caretaker remains in the hands of the Town Council". And that was that...or was it? For in that same year, the Church of Scotland's Property and Endowments Board broached the question of the position (for which read ownership) of the Cathedral, ostensibly to bring it into line with its other properties, or, more cynically, to take complete possession of a building it had effectively been running for over three hundred years, and which was now well worth having. A Writ was served on the Council by the Church of Scotland regarding the ownership of the building, this being answered by the Council, whose case was made ably and well. By March 1929, a Special Meeting of the Council sees the signing of an agreement, and peace reigns once more.

The 1920s saw the tenure of Mr Tait as Caretaker, superseded by Mr John Keldie. By this time, the visitor traffic had apparently increased: in July 1934, this wonderful letter from the Minister, the Reverend William Barclay, to W.J. Heddle, the Town Clerk, was considered at a Town Council meeting:

"As Minister of the Cathedral (the custody of which is in the hands of your Council), and as one jealous of its care, its dignity and its honour, I write to protest most vehemently against the vandalism and desecration which have once again taken place within its sacred walls. I refer, as you may know, to incidents which took place there on Wednesday 11th July, when several hundreds of excursionists were brought from Thurso to Scapa on the St Clair.

On a previous occasion, after a similar exhibition of complete lack of breeding, correspondences ran rife in our local press and in other newspapers with reference to the irreverence and indecency of some of these excursionists in the hope that your Council would take such drastic steps as to prevent a repetition of such in the future, I reluctantly held my peace.

That, however, I can no longer do as the vandalism and desecration which took place on the Thursday holiday 'Out-Herods Herod'.

Is your Council aware that electric lamp guards were forcibly wrenched from the wall, smashed and left at the foot of the stairway while the lamps themselves were either smashed to pieces or removed as souvenirs?

Is your Council aware that the Bell Tower was once again used as a place of public convenience and that the behaviour on the stairway leading to the Tower was outside the bounds of decency?

I have visited many Scottish and English Cathedrals as well as some of the finest in Europe and never once have I seen amongst the hundreds of tourists so much as an act of irreverence, let alone vandalism and desecration. Such would not be tolerated for one moment and yet in ours, 'the wonder and glory of all the North', we still have annual exhibitions of such..."

The Reverend Barclay goes on to commend the Council for the appointment of two assistant caretakers for Mr Keldie, whom he describes as "the guide and custodian", though he questions their combined effectiveness when confronted with "a mob of men quite evidently C.3. both mentally and morally as the perpetrators of the crime of July 11th must have been...", and suggests drastic measures, namely a revision of the notion of admission to the Cathedral Tower, and special regulations to be drawn up for days like the Thurso holiday "which in the opinion of the custodian demand such". Further respectful suggestions from the Reverend Barclay, who had obviously been comparing notes with the custodian were:

"1. That no admission be given to the Cathedral Tower.

2. That admission be given on the payment of 1/-, the money thereby drawn to be expended on the payment of three assistants for the stairway.

3. That admittance to the Cathedral Tower be only at certain stated hours when a guide will take parties of not more than ten to the top, remain with them ten minutes and then escort them as a party to the foot of the stairway."

That the Minister and the Custodian were in concert on this

matter is evident, the next letter discussed being from the Caretaker to the Town Clerk:

"Dear Sir, Some years ago, as the result of the conduct of certain classes of visitors to St Magnus Cathedral, especially those from Caithness and those who turn up at the Lammas Market, I was granted the help of two assistants whenever I thought I required them. Since then, however, I have frequently found this to be inadequate..."

Mr Keldie goes on to list the damage and the outrage: "...I also found that the belfry had been used as a urinal...", and suggests that an additional assistant be posted there and another on the balcony of the south transept, along with a restriction on the number of visitors allowed upstairs. The Council agreed to adopt numbers 2 and 3 of the Reverend Barclay's suggestions, though amended to a tower admission charge of sixpence and fifteen minutes allowed at the top, all only applicable on these special occasions when extra assistance was required...

The remainder of the 1930's saw the Town Hall and Cathedral Committee investigating the state of the heating of the building, apparently not satisfactory on several Sundays. The Caretaker was asked for an explanation and it was agreed that the Depute Town Clerk take temperature readings for a few Sundays, and report back. About eighteen months later, in August 1938, the Provost reported that it had been necessary to suspend the Caretaker, though after consideration, it was decided to reinstate him on probation for six months. It was also decided that the Town Hall and Cathedral Committee should visit the Cathedral occasionally, and a rota was drawn up.

The problem of large groups of visitors, or rather, who should look after them on a Sunday, arose again in July 1938, after a visit by the German cruise liner *Berlin*. The Clerk was instructed to inform the Reverend Mr Fryer that the Council's Caretaker would take charge of such visitors on a Sunday, in terms of the Agreement in regard to the Cathedral. Curiously, less than one year later, in May 1939, the Provost and Magistrates, as Trustees of the Thoms Bequest, are recommending a cut in wages of £12 per annum for this apparently indispensible individual. However good sense on the part of the Council prevailed, and it was agreed, in June 1939, that no reduction be made.

It would appear that the war years concentrated minds greatly,

South transept chapel.

but by 1946, the monthly inspection of the Cathedral by the Town Hall and Cathedral Committee is back in force. In 1948, plans for the automatic ringing of the curfew are proposed, and the Custodian's half-day is moved from Wednesday to Tuesday during the summer months, "owing to the later sailing of the Shetland Steamer".

In May 1955, it would appear that the Cathedral Custodian was becoming more of a Council man, being placed on the Superannuation Scheme, though the Thoms Bequest is still asked to contribute to his salary. By November 1957, his salary was raised, the contribution from the Thoms Trust remaining unaltered, but the Council did not attach any special significance to the increase in tourist traffic, presumably used as a reason for requesting more money, "...as the conduct of visitors round the cathedral is a normal part of his duties..."

1958 saw suggestions that the Church of Scotland should share in the heating and cleaning of the Cathedral, that a Society of Friends be formed, and a chapel to St Rognvald is proposed, subject to Kirk Session approval. Assistants to the Cathedral Caretaker (note how frequently the title changes...!) must have been thin on the ground, for in that year the Town Clerk reported that the Cathedral Caretaker, Mr Albert Thomson, had been giving instruction to several senior schoolboys who would be capable of acting in pairs as holiday relief to him. The Council agreed to this, and to the weekly amount that the caretaker received being shared between the boys, "...as they may themselves agree". A different age indeed...

By November 1960, however, all was not well with Council and Kirk relations at Cathedral level again, for we see the Council's man tendering his resignation as "curator" of St Magnus Cathedral from Saturday, 7th January, 1961. However, it was decided that a Committee consisting of the Provost and two senior magistrates should meet with Mr A. Thomson and members of the Kirk Session "to discuss the position."

Thus, towards the end of the month, the Committee met with the Reverend J.M. Rose and two other members representing the Kirk Session, and with Mr Thomson. Apparently a "full and frank" discussion on "difficulties which have arisen" ensued, concluding with a joint agreement on the following, presumably the reasons for the Custodian tendering his resignation:

No visitors to be allowed up the tower on Sundays.

No-one should be allowed up the tower on Sundays, save for bell-ringers and visitors with an interest in bell-ringing.

Exceptions to this were any party authorised by either the Minister or the Custodian of the Cathedral.

These measures and a rise in salary effected the withdrawal of the Custodian's notice of resignation, though the whole affair serves to highlight, again, the potential for argument when two bodies are running a building. Also, the conclusion may have been something of a Pyrrhic victory for the Custodian, for one month later there was further Council discussion on the recent agreement, it being emphasised that "the compromise arrangements "were not to be regarded as a binding decision on the rights of the two parties agreed in 1929...

In January 1962, the Scottish Community Drama Association (Orkney District), obviously a body with a fine sense of location, proposed to perform T. S. Elliot's verse drama "Murder in the Cathedral". There were no objections on the part of the Council, provided the Kirk Session approved.

An increase in the secular use of the building was evident in the 1960s: Mr Cruikshank, the Kirkwall Grammar School music teacher, was allowed to take parties of senior pupils "for lectures at the organ", the times to be agreed with the Custodian. The Choral Union and Kirkwall Amateur Orchestra were given permission to practise in the Cathedral prior to their May 1965 concert, and there was no objection to their proposed admission charge of 2/6d. Extra guides, with the Cathedral to be open all day, was to be the norm during the "Devonia" educational cruises, with the necessary arrangements being made by the Custodian. Floodlighting the building was proposed, this to be gradually installed, and information notices, "in keeping with the dignity of the building" were to be obtained. In all, it would appear that the Town Council were becoming very aware of the value of their inheritance, and of the need to keep it in order. Perhaps the role of the Custodian was also acknowledged to be changing, for he was now to be given leave entitlement applicable to administrative staff, though he was still allowed to make arrangements for his own relief.

And were relations between the representatives of Council and Kirk improving? Certainly at one level, for the Moderator and

Session Clerk of St Magnus Cathedral, writing on behalf of the Kirk Session, expressed "the sense of indebtedness and gratitude" for the assistance given by the Council in the installation of supplementary heating...

If the 1960s saw increasing concern on the part of the Town Council with the care and running of the building, the 1970s saw positive action towards preservation, and a great increase in the public and secular use of the Cathedral. The Society of Friends launched an appeal fund in January 1972, in order to help with the costs of the structural stabilisation of the building, though by this time the organ had been rebuilt and the heating system upgraded, and the Cathedral had survived a minor fire, caused by a floodlight on the SE triforium roof. The cost of all this was evidently worrying someone: the "Kirkwall Citizen's Association" enquired "as to the position regarding the possibility of the Crown taking over St Magnus Cathedral", presumably in order to avoid the cost of the maintenance. And as in 1851, this was concluded to be legally impossible "as long as the building continues to be used for ecclesiastical purposes," and this was duly noted. Later that year, the Kirkwall Citizen's Association again concerned themselves with the Cathedral, this time expressing their concern that vibration from the Power Station may be affecting the structural stability of the Cathedral, though this was refuted by the Hydro. However, the matter was passed to the architect supervising, Mr Heward.

In January 1973, the Cathedral Custodian was awarded the British Empire Medal, the Town Council expressing pleasure "at the acknowledgement of the services of "Mr Albert J. Thomson", and the Town Clerk and Chamberlain was instructed to write to him conveying the congratulations of the Council. Arrangements were made to hold the Investiture in the Cathedral, after the Kirking of the Council on Sunday, May 6th, with the Council and guests of the Provost meeting in the Council Chambers after the service, for "a pre-lunch refreshment."

With the increase of high profile religious and secular events and performances in the Cathedral, a trend begun in the 1960s, we see the Custodian enquiring of the Town Clerk and Chamberlain as to who was responsible for "the safe keeping" of the Cathedral during such performances. Almost amazingly, the conclusion was that the organisers of these events should be responsible for

Willie Groat ringing the peal of three bells.

Custodian Albert Thomson BEM, ringing the curfew bell.

opening, safety precautions, and the closing of the Cathedral...

By 1974, the big event was Local Government Reform, with the demise of Kirkwall Town Council in favour of the new Islands Authority to take place the following year. The position of the ownership and the administration of the Cathedral now became a matter for concern, with the Session Clerk writing to organise a meeting with Town Council, Kirk and County Council members on this forthcoming issue. There were three main points raised, these being:

a. Does management of the Cathedral transfer to the new Islands Authority?

b. If not, what happens to the functions carried out at present by the Town Council?

c. What could be the alternatives?

The County Clerk, Mr Graeme Lapsley, was formally asked by the Town Council to act on their behalf with legal agents in Edinburgh. The 1486 Charter and subsequent amendments were again examined, with legal opinion being that there should not be a problem in transfer, though any changes should be ratified by Act of Parliament. There was apparently a reluctance on the part of the new Islands Council (January 1975), to take on the Cathedral, though it became acknowledged that there was no practical alternative. It was then agreed to recommend that the Town Council ask the new Orkney Islands Council to "give careful attention to the constitution of the Committee or Sub-Committee of that Council which will manage or advise of the management of the Cathedral after reform of Local Government."

In the meantime, Cathedral life continued, and at an accelerating pace. May 1975 had seen the last meeting of the Town Council and the advent of Orkney Islands Council. In 1976, the Kirkwall Flower Arrangement Club request and are granted sole use of the building for their displays at the time of the St Magnus Fair, a revival of the old Lammas Fair, and now an established fund-raiser for the Cathedral. The following year it agreed to support the first St Magnus Festival, with a performance in the Cathedral of "The Martyrdom of St Magnus" - a collaboration between the composer Peter Maxwell Davies and the Orcadian writer George Mackay Brown. Visitors were very much on the increase, and the St Magnus Cathedral Committee of Orkney Islands Council decided that a register of cruise visits be kept and information on these obtained from the Dept. of Harbours, the Tourist Office, and local shipping agents, so that appropriate arrangements could be made with "the Curator of the cathedral" to ensure that there was no conflict in the use of the building. It was also proposed to open the building in the evening during the summer months.

Perhaps the growing importance of the Cathedral is best seen in the decision to append the secular running of the building to the Chief Executive's office, the Custodian answering to him.

Major structural repairs were now nearing completion, and it was decided to set up a system whereby the Custodian would notify the Chief Architectural Officer of everyday maintenance repairs, and would keep a record of the work done. Plans to employ a Cathedral mason were made, though this post was not filled until the mid-1980s. The Custodian, Mr Thomson, was due to retire in August 1978, and it was decided to take on an assistant, Mr John Windwick, to be trained up towards replacing him.

Restoration workers in the 1970s, with custodian Albert Thomson B.E.M.

The increase in secular events in the Cathedral, notably the regular use by the St Magnus Festival and the schools, prompted the suggestion that the Kirk Session might be asked to provide guidelines "to ensure that these [events] did not detract from the dignity of the building as a place of worship", and also that such users would make a suitable donation to the Appeal Fund, in recognition of the facilities made available to them.

The 1970s set the tone for the 1980s use of the Cathedral and re-defined and expanded the role of the Custodian. The 1990s saw the Cathedral with a permanent staff of a Custodian, his assistant, and two relief custodians. A stone-mason and an assistant had been appointed in the 1980s, which took the maintenance of the fabric away from the Custodian.

The present-day Custodian and his assistants now cater for a regular tourist clientele, and visitor numbers are estimated to be well in excess of fifty-five thousand per year. There are regular events held in the building during all seasons, all of which demand a high level of prescience and liaison with the various parties involved, including working closely with the Kirk. Present personnel handle everything from royal visits to ensuring that the lost visitor gets on the right bus, from making sure that the telephone is disconnected before a wedding service to listening to reminiscences of ex-servicemen returning to visit a building they once were in some fifty years before...and there are no reasons to suspect that our predecessors would have done it otherwise.

MAJOR BEQUESTS AND FUNDING

Tom Muir

St Magnus Cathedral has benefited from two important bequests, separated from each other by one hundred years. In 1805 Gilbert Laing Meason bequeathed £1000, the interest from which was to be used for the upkeep and adornment of the building. Meason was the son of Robert Laing of Strenzie, a former provost of Kirkwall, but had adopted the surname of Meason from his father's business partner who had left him his fortune. He was a brother of the historian Malcolm Laing of Papdale and Samuel Laing, the writer and translator of the saga *Heimskringla*.

The Thoms Bequest provoked this response from some who feared the over-restoration of the Cathedral.

By the mid 19th century the fabric of the building was in a poor state of repair. In 1845 it was claimed by the Government through Her Majesty's Woods and Forest Commissioners, who had inherited the Bishopric lands in Orkney and wrongly thought that this included the Cathedral. The congregation was evicted, as it was intended that the building would be restored and retained as an ancient monument. Restoration went ahead, but in 1850 the magistrates and Town Council reasserted their claim to the Cathedral. After a lengthy debate the Government gave up their claim to the building, informing Provost James Spence of their decision in a letter dated 13th November 1851. All work that had been carried out was gratefully acknowledged as a donation.

Queen Elizabeth the Queen Mother, Patron to the Society of the Friends of St Magnus Cathedral, with Provost Flett.   (photo - W. J. Hourston)

George Hunter Thoms was born in Dundee in 1831, and served as Sheriff for Orkney, Caithness and Zetland from 1870-99. On his death on 25th October 1903 he left an estate worth over £80,000. He had been an eccentric yet generous man, giving 500 acres of land in Dundee in 1896 for the foundation of the Morgan Hospital. He also had a memorial window placed in St Mary's Parish Church, Dundee. In his will he left money to the Orkney and Zetland Association, the Society of Antiquaries of Scotland, his valet, and St Giles Cathedral, Edinburgh. The greatest part of his estate, not to exceed £60,000, was left to St Magnus Cathedral, for its restoration and for the insertion of memorial glass in the existing rose window at its east end.

His two nephews, who had been left only a pair of screens and a gong, contested the will, saying that their uncle was of unsound mind. In a very public legal case, which was published in The Orkney Herald on 13th July 1904, they cited some of their uncle's eccentric behaviour:

"He used to carry a pair of tawse in his pocket and apply them to the children of his friends and relatives. He had elaborate rules printed for the guidance of his domestic servants, and imposed fines for infraction thereof, and also fined himself if he committed any breach of them. He also imposed fines on a favourite cat called "Sambo" if it disturbed the order of the house. He kept what he called a laughing waistcoat with elastic sides, which he wore when out dining."

Another eccentricity recorded was that he had decided that he was the Chief of the Clan McThomas of Glenshee, and had adopted the name as a second middle name. This claim was not based on any evidence. One of his legal documents, dated 21st March 1893, stated that he was to be buried in St Giles Cathedral, Edinburgh, "...in a wicker or other slight coffin, so as to have a chance to begin early at the general scramble at the resurrection."

The nephews lost the case, and St Magnus Cathedral was left with a considerable sum of money to fund major restorations, carried out between 1913 -30.

In 1958 the Society of the Friends of St Magnus Cathedral was formed to raise funds for the care of the Cathedral. In 1971 they were horrified to learn that major structural faults had been detected in the west end of the building. Another near disaster occurred that same year when part of the presbytery roof was set alight by an electrical fault, damaging an area of 200 square feet. A major fund-raising campaign was launched to save the Cathedral, including the inauguration of the annual St Magnus Fair held in August. Her Royal Highness Queen Elizabeth the Queen Mother consented to become Patron to the Society of the Friends of St Magnus Cathedral, and also made a contribution to the funds. A special Service of Thanksgiving was held on 7th August 1974 to celebrate the saving of the Cathedral and the raising of £100,000 towards the cost of repairs. It was attended by Queen Elizabeth the Queen Mother, along with some 700 people. The Society of the Friends of St Magnus Cathedral is still raising funds, as repair and maintenance is a never ending process.

First visit, in 1960, of Queen Elizabeth II and the Duke of Edinburgh by Stanley Cursiter R.S.A., P.R.S.W., Queen's Limner and Painter in Scotland.